Photo by T. Charles Erickson

A scene from the McCarter Theatre production of "Having Our Say." Set design by Thomas Lynch.

HAVING OUR SAY

The Delany Sisters' First 100 Years

A PLAY BY

EMILY MANN

ADAPTED FROM THE BOOK BY
SARAH L. DELANY AND
A. ELIZABETH DELANY
WITH
AMY HILL HEARTH

DRAMATISTS
PLAY SERVICE
INC.

2

This play is dedicated to the memory of two extraordinary fathers,
Bishop Henry Beard Delany
and
Professor Arthur Mann

My special thanks to
producers Judith Rutherford James and Camille O. Cosby
to my sister, Carol Mann
and of course
to
Dr. Bessie Delany, Miss Sadie Delany,
and Amy Hill Hearth

HAVING OUR SAY The Delany Sisters' First 100 Years received its premiere at the McCarter Theatre (Emily Mann, Artistic Director; Jeffrey Woodward, Managing Director) in Princeton, New Jersey, on February 7, 1995. It was directed by Emily Mann; the set design was by Thomas Lynch; the costume design was by Judy Dearing; the lighting design was by Allen Lee Hughes; the music was composed and arranged by Baikida Carroll; the dramaturg was Janice Paran; the production stage manager was Martin Gold and the stage manager was Ed De Shae. The cast was as follows:

MISS SADIE DELANY .... Gloria Foster
DR. BESSIE DELANY .... Mary Alice

HAVING OUR SAY The Delany Sisters' First 100 Years was subsequently produced on Broadway at the Booth Theatre (Camille O. Cosby and Judith Rutherford James, Producers) in April, 1995. It was directed by Emily Mann; the set design was by Thomas Lynch; the costume design was by Judy Dearing; the lighting design was by Allen Lee Hughes; the music was composed and arranged by Baikida Carroll; the production stage manager was Martin Gold and the stage manager was Ed DeShae. The cast was as follows:

MISS SADIE DELANY .... Gloria Foster
DR. BESSIE DELANY .... Mary Alice

PERFORMANCE NOTES

The actresses speak directly to the audience. The actresses also respond directly to the audience. The audience is as present to the actresses as the actresses are to us. We are, indeed, the visitor.

The sisters often finish each other's sentences, speak in unison, echo each other's thoughts and gestures. After one hundred years of living together, they are, as Sadie says, "in some ways, like one person."

The performance pace is very rapid and highly orchestrated.

In the original production, there were three playing areas: 1) the sitting room, 2) the dining room, 3) the kitchen. Pictures from the Delany sisters' family photo album as well as historical images were projected onto the walls of the frame above them. The set is a memory space.

HAVING OUR SAY

The Delany Sisters' First 100 Years

ACT ONE

Sweet Sadie and Queen Bess

An image of the Delany family home in Mount Vernon, New York fills the space and dissolves. Then, lights come up slowly on Sadie Delany. She stands straight and tall, addressing the audience.

SADIE.   Bessie and I have been together since time began, or so it seems. Bessie is my little sister, only she's not so little. She is 101 years old, and I am 103. *(Bessie enters the dining room, begins setting up a tea tray.)* You know, people always say they'd like to live to be one hundred, but no one really expects to, except Bessie. She always said she planned to be as old as Moses. And when Bessie says she's going to do something, she does it. *(Bessie loads the tray with cups, creamer, sugar. Sadie sits in an easy chair in the sitting room.)* Neither one of us ever married and we've lived together most all of our lives, and probably know each other better than any two human beings on this Earth. After so long, we are in some ways like one person. *(Bessie starts to cross in with tea.)*

BESSIE.   How do you do! I'm Dr. Delany. Make yourself comfortable. Stay as long as you like. We won't charge you rent. *(Bessie puts down the tray, looks to the audience, eyes fiercely penetrating. They both laugh uproariously, then Bessie starts to pour tea.)* Truth is, I never thought I'd see the day when people would be interested in what two old Negro women have to say. Life still surprises me. So maybe the last laugh is on me.

SADIE. You want to talk to us? Are you sure? Well … if you think it will help somebody, then it's worth doing. That's what Mama used to say.

BESSIE. I had a prayer — Lord, send us someone new. Everyone we know is dead or they're boring us to death. *Lord, send us someone new! (Bessie sits.)*

SADIE. *(Joyous.)* Then *you* knocked on the door! *(They both laugh.)* Have some tea, now. Go on! *(Puts sugar in her tea.)* You know, Bessie and I were in helping professions — she was a dentist and I was a high school teacher —

BESSIE. so we're not rich, but we get by.

SADIE. Papa always taught us that with every dollar you earn, the first ten cents goes to the Lord…. The second ten cents —

BESSIE. … goes in the bank for hard times …

SADIE. And the rest is yours, but you better spend it wisely. Well, it's a good thing we listened because we're living on that

BESSIE and SADIE. *(Together.)* hard-time money now,

SADIE. and not doing too badly. We Delanys had everything but money. I remember once, Bessie and me and Julia,

BESSIE. our little sister,

SADIE. made a circle around Papa and said, "Papa … we are going to squeeze a nickel out of you!" And he laughed and said "Go ahead and try, daughters, but

BESSIE and SADIE. *(Together.)* there's no nickel here!"

BESSIE. Our Papa was one of the finest men you could find in America or anywhere else for that matter.

SADIE. Remember he would take us outside and teach us the names of the planets and stars.

BESSIE. Papa knew them all. He was so excited when Halley's Comet came by.

SADIE. He had us all outside that night, and it was a sight to see, flickering light across the landscape. I remember Papa saying, "I don't think any of us will be here to see Halley's Comet the next time it comes around."

BESSIE. Well, he was wrong about that.

SADIE. Yes he was. We have lived in New York for the last seventy-five years, but Raleigh

8

BESSIE and SADIE. *(Together.)* will always be home.

BESSIE.　Raleigh is where Mama and Papa met, as students at Saint Augustine's School,

SADIE.　which was a school for Negroes.

BESSIE.　That's their picture over there.

SADIE.　They got married in the campus chapel and raised all ten of us children right there at —

BESSIE and SADIE. *(Together.)* good old "Saint Aug's."

BESSIE.　Papa became vice-principal and Mama was the matron, which meant she ran things day-to-day at the school. Our Papa became the first elected Negro bishop of the Episcopal Church, U.S.A.

SADIE.　That's a long way for a man who was born a slave on a Georgia plantation, but if you had known Papa, you wouldn't be surprised. He was always improving himself, and he and Mama brought us up to

BESSIE and SADIE. *(Together.)* reach high.

SADIE.　Mama, who was from Virginia, was an issue-free Negro.

BESSIE.　*(To Sadie.)* Explain what issue free means. *(Before Sadie can answer.)* That's a person who had some Negro blood but whose mother was a free person, not a slave. Mama looked white but she never did try to "pass." She was proud to be a colored woman!

SADIE.　*(Putting down her cup.)* You know — I don't remember life without Bessie. "Queen Bess," as Papa used to call her, was born on

BESSIE.　September 3, 1891. They named me Annie Elizabeth.

SADIE.　I came into this world two years earlier on the nineteenth day of September,

BESSIE and SADIE. *(Together.)* 1889.

BESSIE.　They named her Sarah Louise,

SADIE.　but I've always been called Sadie.

BESSIE.　*(Laughing.)* "Sweet sister Sadie," "sweet sister Sadie," "sweet sister Sadie" ...

SADIE.　*(Gently quiets Bessie.)* Bessie was so alert at birth that Mama said she had a funny feeling that child would have a mind of her own. Bessie was what we used to call a "feeling child"; she was sensitive and emotional. She was quick to anger, and very outspoken.

BESSIE.   And Sadie was a "mama's child."

SADIE.   Yes, I followed my Mama around like a shadow. I always did what I was told. I was calm and agreeable.

BESSIE.   She was shy.

SADIE.   The way I see it, there's room in the world for both me and Bessie. We kind of balance each other out. *(Bessie gets up, pours more tea.)*

BESSIE.   People learned not to mess with me from Day One. *(Sadie adds sugar to her tea.)*

SADIE.   Papa used to say, "You catch more flies with molasses than vinegar."

BESSIE.   Well, that's easy for you to swallow. You are molasses without even trying! See, Sadie can sweet-talk the world, or play dumb, or whatever it takes to get by without a fuss. But even as a tiny little child, I wasn't afraid of anything. I'd meet the Devil before day and look him in the eye, no matter what the price. If Sadie is molasses, then I am vinegar! Sadie is sugar, and I'm the spice. *(Bessie sits.)*

SADIE.   It's a wonder she wasn't lynched.

BESSIE.   Well, I almost was, but that's another story. The thing is I know Sadie's going to get into Heaven, but I'm not so sure about me. I'm working on it, but it sure is hard to change. I've been trying to change for one hundred years without success, that's not so good, is it? I'm afraid when I meet St. Peter at the Gate, he'll say, "Lord, child, you were *mean!*"

SADIE.   She has trouble with the idea of forgiving and forgetting.

BESSIE.   That's right. You see, I can forgive, but I can't seem to forget. And I'm not sure the Lord would approve of that at all. I remember things that happened long, long ago that still make me madder than a hornet. I wish they didn't. Most of the people I'm still mad at are long dead and there are things I can tell you ... *(She stops herself.)* but Sadie will say, "Now Bessie, of the dead —

BESSIE and SADIE.   *(Together.)* ... say nothing Evil."

BESSIE.   So ... I try to be good. But the rebby boys tend to stand out, make themselves known. You don't know what a rebby boy is.

SADIE.   That's what we call white racist men. It's short for rebel.

BESSIE.   I'll tell you, the way those rebby types treat colored folks — well, it just makes me sick. If I had a pet buzzard I'd treat him better than the way some white folks have treated me! There isn't a Negro this side of Glory who doesn't know exactly what I mean. Those rebby types don't give colored folks credit for a thing. They learn early to hate. Why, colored folks *built* this country, and that is the truth. We were the laborers, honey! We were the backbone of this country *(She stops herself.)* Now, Sadie doesn't get all agitated like this. It's been a little harder for me, partly because I'm darker than she is, and the darker you are, honey, the harder it is. But it's also been harder on me because I have a different personality than Sadie. She is a true Christian woman! I wish I were more like her but I'm afraid I am a naughty little darky! Ha ha! *(Bessie laughs.)* I know it's not fashionable to use some of the words from our heyday, but that's who I am! And who is going to stop me? Nobody, that's who! Ain't nobody going to censor *me*, no sir! I'm a hundred-and-one years old and at my age, honey, I can say what I want! *(She gets up and exits into the kitchen.)*

SADIE.   *(Conspiratorial, to audience.)* I'll tell you something about Bessie. Bessie thinks she's a little psychic. I try not to encourage this, because it's ungodly. But over the years I've come to believe that Bessie is a little, well, *intuitive.* And I admit that it often comes in handy. You see, we don't have a telephone. We have to rely on the U.S. mail and on Bessie's intuition. *(Bessie re-enters with tea biscuits.)*

BESSIE.   We *hate* phones!

SADIE.   Of course, we had a phone years ago when Bessie was a practicing dentist. We had to, and that was OK. But ever since we moved to this house, in 1957, we have not had a phone.

BESSIE.   The phone company comes by and pesters us. *(Sits.)*

SADIE.   Finally we told the man, "Mister, if the phone com-

11

pany installed a phone for free and paid for a man to stand there and answer it for us, seven days a week ...

BESSIE and SADIE. *(Together.)* We *still wouldn't want a phone!*

BESSIE. He got the message. *(Bessie laughs.)*

SADIE. And I'll tell you something else about Bessie. *(Bessie looks up, surprised.)* She has made a full-time job out of watching over the whole neighborhood. She's always looking out the window and reporting to me what so-and-so is doing. I say, "Now, Bessie, is that really your business?"

BESSIE. If it's going on in my neighborhood, it's my business.

SADIE. Bessie is a nosy old gal.

BESSIE. I'll tell you about nosy! People are always asking us how we've lived past one hundred. *(She laughs.)* I say, "We never married. We never had husbands to worry us to death!" *(She screams with laughter. They both laugh.)* I love to laugh. Oppressed people have a good sense of humor. Think of the Jews. They know how to laugh,

SADIE. and to laugh at themselves! *(Bessie and Sadie set tea things on tray.)*

BESSIE. Well, we colored folks are the same way. We colored folks are survivors. *(Lights fade as Bessie exits with tea tray and Sadie crosses to pick up a photo album from the book shelf.)*

Saint Aug's

> *Photos of the family from the early part of the last century flood the space and dissolve. Lights up — Sadie is looking through a family album. Bessie enters with a box of pictures, then exits. As the sisters show each picture, it is projected.*

SADIE. You asked us about our family so we thought we'd show you some pictures, get you familiar with who all the faces are. *(Sadie shows photo of Papa from album.)* This is Papa. Born on February 5, 1858. Henry Beard Delany, born into slavery on a plantation owned by the Mock family in St. Mary's, Georgia, on the coast near the Florida border. *(Holding photo album.)* He was just a little bitty fellow — seven years old —

when the Surrender came in 1865. The end of slavery ... *(Bessie enters with second box of photos.)*

BESSIE.   The end of the Civil War! When General Robert E. Lee surrendered to the Union at Appomattox Court House! Now *that* was *surrender! (Bessie sits.)*

SADIE.   We used to ask Papa: "what do you remember about being a slave?" Well, like a lot of former slaves, he didn't say much about it. Everybody had their own tale of woe and for most people, things had been so bad you didn't want to think about it, let alone talk about it.

BESSIE.   You didn't sit and cry in your soup, honey, you just went on. *(Holds a photo of the grandparents.)* This is his father, our grandfather, Thomas Sterling Delany, and this is his mother, our grandmother, Sarah ...

SADIE.   She was obviously part Indian — see — she had long, straight black hair ...

BESSIE.   Remember, we used to giggle about her photograph when we were little ...

SADIE.   Her hair looked so peculiar to us.

BESSIE.   Altogether, Sarah and Thomas had eleven children, and our Papa was the youngest.

SADIE.   Now, what made the big difference for our family was the Mocks broke the Georgia law by teaching Papa and his brothers and sisters to *read* and *write.*

BESSIE.   Education! Education, child. Education always makes the difference!

SADIE.   Papa said the Mocks were very fine people.

BESSIE.   That's a generous thing to say about the people who *owned* him, wouldn't you say?

SADIE.   But he said there was great variety in the way white people treated Negroes, and it's true now, too. *(Bessie begins to remove photos from box.)* The Mocks thought a heap of Sarah and Thomas Delany. Maybe they thought the Delanys wouldn't leave after the Surrender —

BESSIE and SADIE.   *(Together.)* But they did.

BESSIE.   And they didn't have but the shirt on their backs.

SADIE.   Those were hard times, after slavery days.

BESSIE. *(Angry.)* The whites fixed it so those Negroes could never get ahead.

SADIE. You see, the Delanys were among only a *handful* of former slaves in those parts who didn't end up begging. Papa was proud of this, beyond words. They were smart, but they were lucky, and they knew it. They could read and write and hadn't been abused, and their family was still together. That's a lot more than most former slaves had going for them.

BESSIE. Now, one day when Papa was already a grown man down in Florida, a white Episcopal priest —

SADIE. — the Reverend Owen Thackara —

BESSIE. Yes. Reverend Thackara noticed our father had brains, and said to him, "Young man, you should go to college."

SADIE. Well! The Delanys were Methodists through and through, but the idea of college was so fantastic it boggled Papa's mind. He jumped at the chance.

BESSIE. Reverend Thackara helped Papa go to Saint Augustine's School, an Episcopal school way north in Raleigh, in the great state of North Carolina.

SADIE. Papa was a shining star among shining stars. He was as smart as he could be, and blessed with a personality that smoothed the waters. He soon met a fellow student named Nanny James Logan, *(Bessie picks up a photo of Mama.)*

BESSIE. Our Mama —

SADIE. The belle of the campus. She was a pretty gal and very popular despite the fact that she was smarter than all the boys —

BESSIE. Smarter! She was the class valedictorian!

SADIE. Yes, the only reason Papa didn't finish first was because

BESSIE and SADIE. *(Together.)* Mama finished first!

BESSIE. Our Mama! Our Mama was born in Virginia in a community called Yak.

SADIE. Today, they call it Mountain Hill. Guess they think that sounds better than Yak.

BESSIE. Now Mama's people are another story.

SADIE. Oh yes.

BESSIE.   Mama's great-grandmother, Mrs. John Logan, —

SADIE.   who was white —

BESSIE.   Yes — she took up with a slave on her plantation while her husband had gone off to —

BESSIE and SADIE.   *(Together.)* The War of 1812.

BESSIE.   She had two daughters with the slave, and when her husband returned, do you know he *forgave* his wife ...

SADIE.   Forgave her.

BESSIE.   And adopted those two colored girls as his own!? No one knows what happened to the slave except he must have left town in a big hurry.

SADIE.   A big hurry —

BESSIE.   One of those two girls, Eliza Logan *(Shows photo.)*, got involved with a white man named Jordan Motley.

SADIE.   We have a picture of him, too. *(Shows photo.)*

BESSIE.   They had a child, Martha Logan, our grandma *(Shows photo.)*, and three other daughters. Now one thing's for *sure*, even though our grandma and her three sisters were only one-quarter Negro, in the eyes of the world they were colored. So they were in a bind when it came to marrying.

SADIE.   If they wanted to marry a colored man, well most of them were slaves.

BESSIE.   And they couldn't marry white, because it was illegal for Negroes and whites to marry in Virginia.

SADIE.   Until 1967!

BESSIE.   But, it didn't stop them from having love relationships.

SADIE.   No, it didn't. Our grandma took up with a man named James Miliam

BESSIE.   who was as white as he could be and the meanest looking man in Pittsylvania County, Virginia. *(Shows photo.)*

SADIE.   We remember our grandparents well because we used to go visit every summer, and we were young women when they died. They clearly loved each other very much. They lived like man and wife for fifty years and didn't part until death.

BESSIE.   Mr. Miliam built a log cabin for Grandma a few hundred feet from his house.

SADIE. He even built a walkway between the two houses

BESSIE. so he could go see Grandma without getting his boots muddy.

SADIE. Now, this kind of arrangement was unusual between a white man and a colored woman.

BESSIE. More normal was when a white man had a white wife and a colored mistress on the side.

SADIE. But James Miliam had no white wife, and was entirely devoted to grandma.

BESSIE. He put his money where his heart was! Every Sunday, Grandma would walk to the White Rock Baptist Church for services. One time, there was a movement in the church to throw her out, on account of her relationship with Mr. Miliam. But one of the deacons stood up and defended her. He reminded the congregation that those two would have been legally married if they could.

SADIE. And that those two were committed to each other — a lot more so than some of the married people in the congregation.

BESSIE. And anyway, James Miliam couldn't help being white. So, they let Grandma keep coming to that church. One summer — you and I were there, remember? — Grandma told Mama, "Soon my time to die will be coming." She told Mama to have some of us grand-children stay with Mr. Miliam when we could, because he would be lonely without her.

SADIE. Poor Mr. Miliam. When Grandma died, we saw him — he sat in Grandma's kitchen with his head in his big hands and he said, "What I loved most in this world is lying in the other room." So Bessie and I stayed, cooked and kept him company.

BESSIE. In the morning, Mr. Miliam would go out and shoot a squirrel for his breakfast. He always used to say: "those little ones are mighty tasty."

SADIE. Grandma had predicted Mr. Miliam would not last long without her, and she was right. Despite our efforts to keep him happy, he died just two years after Grandma.

BESSIE. The will was challenged by some white nephew of his who was just furious over the fact that our Mama, "this colored woman," should get those 68 acres and that money ... even if·she was Mr. Miliam's *daughter!*

SADIE.   Mama gave $500 to the nephew to keep the fellow happy. She didn't want to be sued. But she did what Mr. Miliam would have wanted.

BESSIE and SADIE.   *(Together.)* She hung onto that land.

SADIE.   And to this day, it is *still* in our family.

BESSIE.   Those white relatives are just waiting for us to mess up, *just once* with those taxes. Be one day late. But we haven't. Not in 85 years. And we won't. *(Bessie stands.)* That land is ...

BESSIE and SADIE.   *(Together. Shaking hands.)* ... *ours. (Bessie crosses for glass of water on the dining room table.)*

BESSIE.   Our Mama was always a bit embarrassed that her parents were not — could not have been — legally married. She was determined that she was going to have a legal marriage someday, or not get married at all!

SADIE.   And she got her pick of beaus at Saint Aug's! And it didn't matter to her in the least that her favorite was a lot darker than she was.

BESSIE.   Some colored women who were as light as Mama would not have gotten involved with a dark-skinned man, but Mama didn't care.

SADIE.   She said he was the cream of the crop, a man of the highest quality.

BESSIE.   Oh, Mama was a smart woman.

SADIE.   It takes a smart woman to fall in love with a good man.

BESSIE.   Our Papa felt the same way about her.

SADIE.   Papa's parents presented him with this Bible in which he wrote: *(Opens the Bible.)* "Given to Henry Beard Delany by his parents upon graduating from college." Then, he took the train right back to Raleigh and he married Miss Nanny James Logan at the Saint Aug's chapel on the 6th of October, 1886. *(Bessie picks up baby picture of Lemuel and shows audience.)*

BESSIE.   Lemuel, our oldest brother, arrived the next year. Lemuel Thackara.

SADIE.   He was named after the white Episcopal priest who helped Papa go to college.

17

BESSIE. We were all named after somebody!

SADIE. We have a picture of the whole family, in about — *(Sadie crosses to photo and picks it up. She shows it to the audience.)*

BESSIE. 1906.

SADIE. Yes. 1906. Every two years there was a new baby: Lemuel, me, then Bessie, then

BESSIE and SADIE. *(Together.)* Julia, Hap, Lucius, Manross, Hubert, Laura, and Samuel Ray.

SADIE. See baby Sam in Mama's arms? That's our house at St. Aug's in the background there. You know, it always seemed like somebody was knocking on our door, looking for food when we were small. Mama never turned anyone away.

BESSIE. No she didn't.

SADIE. She'd stop whatever she was doing and fix them a plate.

BESSIE. Hunger was a big problem for former slaves.

SADIE. Most of these folks just went on their way, though one, a man named

BESSIE and SADIE. *(Together.)* Jesse Edwards ...

SADIE. Mr. Jesse Edwards stayed for ten years. He became like a part of our family.

BESSIE. Uncle Jesse. Uncle Jesse had been a slave. Papa gave him the job of carrying the mail.

SADIE. And he took that job seriously!

BESSIE. That old fella never had it so good. Now as poor Uncle Jesse got older — he got a little scrappy. Like sometimes, we would have to go to his old farmhouse and clean it out.

SADIE. A lot of former slaves were like that — they'd never owned anything, so they hung on to all kinds of junk they didn't know what to do with.

BESSIE. *(Refers to photo album.)* This is a picture of our brother, Sam, with Uncle Jesse's house in the background. Do we have a photo of Uncle Jesse? Oh, here's a picture of Mama teaching her cooking class. *(Shows photo from album to Sadie.)*

SADIE. Oh my yes.... I just don't know how she did it all. Mama was really a working mother with a job outside the home. She was the matron and teacher too. But she always had time for us.

BESSIE.   She *made* time for us.

SADIE.   Her day always started long before dawn, and every night she bathed all ten of us in a tin tub which she had to

BESSIE and SADIE.   *(Together.)* fill by hand.

SADIE.   I used to get so tired waiting for my turn because I was the second-oldest child and she would start with the youngest. I don't know why Mama was so concerned about bathing us every day, except that people used to say that Negroes were dirty people and she may have been trying to combat that image.

BESSIE.   Well, we must have been the cleanest children anyone ever saw.. *(Spotting a photo in the album.)* Look! A picture of Professor Boyer teaching you Greek ...

SADIE.   *(Looking at photo.)* Oh, yes ... Professor Boyer.... Why I haven't thought about him in about 100 years...! Where was I? Oh, yes ... after each of us had our bath, we would go into Papa's study where he would read to us from the Bible.

BESSIE.   Papa *edited* the Bible.

SADIE.   Yes, he'd only read the stories he thought we should hear. I didn't know there were stories in the Bible about adultery and things of that nature until I was a grown girl. Why, I thought it was the Good Book! *All good!*

BESSIE.   Each morning, Papa would make us line up for our "inspection." He'd look us over to see if our shoes were polished, our ears were clean, things like that.

SADIE.   We carried the Delany name and he wanted us to look respectable when we left the house.

BESSIE.   That is right.

SADIE.   He never whipped us but once ...

BESSIE.   Sadie!

SADIE.   and only once ...

BESSIE.   Sadie, you're not going to tell this!

SADIE.   When Bessie and I were children.

BESSIE.   Lord! I can't sit still for this! Excuse me. *(Bessie exits into kitchen.)*

SADIE.   He spotted us in a grove far from where we were supposed to go. We hadn't snuck down there on purpose, we just forgot and kind of wandered down there. Well, Papa was just very upset. He was afraid we could have been molested. I guess we were about six and eight years old. He told us to get switches from the peach tree. While we were doing that I whispered to Bessie, "Now, let's don't cry, no matter how many times he hits us!" Bessie agreed, and volunteered to go first with the whipping. Papa whipped her little shoulders and the backs of her legs, and of course, she did not cry. The whipping went on and on, and she did not cry. Finally, Papa quit and said, "Go on, you stubborn little mule." Now it came my turn and after seeing what Bessie had gone through I changed my mind about not crying. So I howled at the very first lash, and one lash was all I got. I'm into surviving, and I can see when I'm licked. What's the sense in getting licked if you don't have to? *(Bessie enters.)*

BESSIE.   I am still mad at you over that whipping incident! It was your idea not to cry in the first place. Well, I would rather die than back down, and that is the truth. See, I take after Mama's people. Mama could be very feisty, and somehow, like me, she lived to tell about it. I remember once how Mama got mad at some white man who wanted to use our telephone. He called Mama "auntie" —

SADIE.   Which was one of the put-down ways white people referred to colored women.

BESSIE and SADIE.   *(Overlap.)* They call men "uncle" or "boy."

BESSIE.   Mama told that man, "You may use my phone, but you may not call me auntie. I am no kin to you." Now, that was a very courageous thing for a colored woman to do in those days.

SADIE.   Yes it was.

BESSIE.   Papa would have let it slide.

SADIE.   It was not in Papa's nature to make a fuss.

BESSIE.   That's right, so it was very difficult for him to whip us that day.

SADIE.   That's right.

BESSIE.   And he had a lot of pride. He really believed in presenting yourself to the world in a dignified fashion. I think that's why he was unhappy about my pet pig, Retta. You see, Retta was the runt of the litter, cast aside and left to die. Well, I took that little piglet and I fed him with a bottle and fussed over him like a baby. Before I knew it, he weighed five hundred pounds. Wherever Sadie and I went, Retta wasn't far behind.

SADIE.   I don't think Papa thought it was fitting for a Delany child to be wandering around the campus of St. Augustine's School followed by a big grunting bull pig.

BESSIE.   One day, Retta bit a man in his privates and that was the end of my poor pig. I imagine he was turned into bacon, and his fat used to make soap. It pains me to this day, because I loved that old pig.

SADIE.   Our childhood years were very protected. Why, we didn't have but the vaguest notion of what sex was. We had a neighbor who said to us once, "You girls are so green, it's a wonder those cows don't mistake you for grass and gobble you up."

BESSIE.   Mmm-hm. I would see the rooster worrying the hen and I'd just go out and beat him. I thought he had no right! It wasn't until years later, when I was teaching school in Brunswick, Georgia, that I finally figured out what this sex stuff was all about from hearing the other teachers talking rather explicitly about sex and men, and I thought, Lord have mercy! Those girls would say, "Come on out with us tonight, Bessie." But I didn't take tea for the fever! If it wasn't right, I wouldn't do it.

SADIE.   *(Laughing.)* I remember once being in a car with Bessie and one of her beaus. He was just beside himself, and he said, real exasperated, "How come you gals never married? Don't y'all know what you're missing?" And I said, "Well ... you don't miss what you don't know." And he nearly went off the road! He yelled, "You do miss it!"

BESSIE and SADIE.   *(Together.)* "You do! You do!"

SADIE.   I thought — well — it must be pretty good, whatever it is. *(They scream with laughter. Bessie starts putting pictures back in the box.)*

BESSIE. We lived a clean life, but Lord, we had a good time. Every one of us children played an instrument — flute, violin, trombone, clarinet — and as a family we formed a band. Some mornings, people would walk past our house and say, "Y'all had a party last night." And we'd say, "Wasn't no party! Was just the bunch of us being musical!"

SADIE. Our Papa was a grand man! He was extremely talented at music and played the organ beautifully, and when he thought no one was around, he'd play and sing these old Methodist hymns from his boyhood.

BESSIE. Episcopalians did not have hymns like those old Methodists. He'd play "Amazing Grace." *(She sings a bar. Sadie hums with her.)* Things like that.

SADIE. I didn't realize it at the time, but I think he missed his people down in Florida. And when he'd play their Methodist hymns, he felt closer to them.

BESSIE. All of the values that made us strong came from the church.

SADIE. Yes, it was religious faith that formed the backbone of the Delany family. We were good Christians, and God never let us down. *(Bessie gets up with box of photographs.)*

BESSIE. I'll tell you something else, honey. We were good citizens! Good Americans. We loved our country, even though it didn't always love us back. *(Slow fade to black as Bessie exits with the box of photographs.)*

END OF ACT ONE

ACT TWO

Jim Crow

The stage floods with images of early Jim Crow (1896): Colored only signs, separate seats in trolleys, water fountains, hospitals and schools. The Delany sisters stare at the photo album, very solemn. Lights up as Bessie crosses to her chair and sits.

SADIE.   America has not ever been able to undo the mess created by those Jim Crow laws.

BESSIE.   The beginning of Jim Crow in North Carolina was the day that everything changed.

SADIE.   We already knew we were second-class citizens but those Jim Crow laws set it in stone.

BESSIE.   At that time, many white people didn't think Negroes had souls. They wanted to believe that.

SADIE.   And powerful white people were getting more and more nervous with the way colored people, after the Civil War, were beginning to get their piece of the pie.

BESSIE.   The pecking order was like this: white men were the most powerful, followed by white women.

SADIE.   Colored people were absolutely below them

BESSIE.   and if you think it was hard for colored men, honey, colored women were on the *bottom*. Yes, sir! Colored women took it from all angles!

SADIE.   You see, a lot of this Jim Crow mess was about sex —

BESSIE.   Yes, some of this race mixing that was going on was left over from slavery days, because white men would often molest their slave women.

SADIE.   But a lot of this racial mixing was just attraction between people, plain and simple, just like happened in our family, on Mama's side. Now, Mama and Papa knew these laws were coming, of course, but they didn't prepare us. Maybe they couldn't explain it ...

BESSIE.   We encountered Jim Crow laws for the first time on a summer Sunday afternoon.

SADIE.   We were about five and seven years old at the time.

BESSIE.   Like in this picture. *(Shows album to Sadie. We see photo of family, beautifully dressed in their Sunday best around 1898.)*

SADIE.   There was a place in Raleigh not just for whites but for the whole city, called Pullen Park.

BESSIE.   Mama and Papa used to take us to Pullen Park for picnics, and that particular day, the trolley driver told us to go to the back.

SADIE.   We children objected loudly, because we always liked to sit in front ...

BESSIE.   ... because the breeze

BESSIE and SADIE.   *(Together.)* would blow our hair. *(They gesture with their hands.)*

SADIE.   That was part of the fun.

BESSIE.   But Mama and Papa just gently told us to hush and took us to the back without making a fuss.

SADIE.   When we got to Pullen Park, we found changes there, too. The spring where you got water now had a big wooden sign across the middle. *(They gesture with their hands.)*

BESSIE.   On one side, the word "white" was painted,

SADIE.   and on the other, the word "colored." What in the world was all this about?

BESSIE.   We may have been little children but, honey, we got the message loud and clear.

SADIE.   *(Laughing.)* But when nobody was looking, Bessie took the tin dipper and leaned over and scooped some water from the other side and said, "I'm goin' get me some *white* water!"

BESSIE.   It tasted just the same. *(They laugh. A beat. Sadie stands, crosses to us. Bessie stands to join her.)*

SADIE.   Today is Papa's birthday. Every year on his birthday, we cook his favorite birthday meal, just the way he liked it:

BESSIE and SADIE.   *(Together.)* chicken and gravy,

SADIE.   rice and sweet potatoes, ham,

BESSIE and SADIE.   *(Together.)* macaroni and cheese,

SADIE.   cabbage,

BESSIE and SADIE.   *(Together.)* cauliflower, broccoli,

BESSIE.   turnips, and carrots.

SADIE.   For dessert we have a birthday cake — a pound cake —

BESSIE and SADIE.   *(Together.)* and ambrosia,

SADIE.   made with oranges and fresh coconut.

BESSIE.   Some people grieve to remember, but we celebrate. Why, we thank the Lord for our Papa everyday!

SADIE.   Oh, please don't go — Bessie and I love to talk while we work. *(Sadie moves towards dining room. The stage slowly revolves. Bessie follows. The table is about to be set with exquisite but simple taste — perfectly pressed linens, etc.)* Why, all we do is talk about folks who turned to dust so long ago that we're the only people on this earth with any memory of them. *(They unfold the tablecloth which rests on the table.)*

BESSIE.   I was just thinking how fortunate it was for Sadie and me that our earliest experiences with whites predated Jim Crow.

SADIE.   Miss Grace Moseley ...

BESSIE.   Oh, remember ...

SADIE.   She was our favorite. She had come to Saint Aug's to teach, along with her mother ...

BESSIE.   Those two were the cream of the crop, child.

SADIE.   They were very fine, cultured white women, from a good family and with the best manners and education.

BESSIE.   Miss Moseley didn't like it that at Saint Aug's the white teachers lived separately from the colored.

SADIE.   She wanted to live with *us.*

BESSIE.   So, every Wednesday evening Miss Moseley would invite Sadie and me, and our little sister Julia, to her living quarters. *(Sadie takes out napkins, Bessie takes out silverware and begins to set it.)*

SADIE.   We would all pile on her bed and she would read us Shakespeare and all the classics. Julia was so little she would fall asleep, but Bessie and I would just snuggle up with Miss

Moseley and she would read to us. That is a lovely memory I carry with me, and it makes me smile to this day. These are Mama's linens. Our favorite serving pieces are Mama's, too. They're up there. They're wedding pieces. Mama never had silver, but before Bessie retired, she bought me a set of silver plate. Isn't she a sweet sister?

BESSIE.   Knowing people like Miss Moseley and our white grandfather, Mr. Miliam, made this Jim Crow mess seem mighty puzzling. *(Bessie lays dinner plates.)*

SADIE.   Yes it did, but I'll tell you how I handled Jim Crow. There was a shoe store in Raleigh called Heller's. The owner was a Jewish man, very nice. If you were colored, you had to go in the back to try on shoes, and the white people sat in the front. It wasn't Mr. Heller's fault; this was the Jim Crow law. I would go in there and say, "Good morning, Mr. Heller, I would like to try on those shoes in the window." And he would say, "That's fine, Miss Delany, go on and sit in the back." And I would say, "Where, Mr. Heller?" And he would say, "Back there." And I would say, "Back *where?*" Well, I'd just worry that man to death. Finally, he'd say, "Just sit anywhere, Miss Delany!" *(Sadie sits.)* And so I would sit myself down in the white section, and smile.

BESSIE.   Lord! I hate when you play dumb like that! *(Sadie laughs, starts to set goblets.)* Every time I encountered prejudice which was rubbed in my face under Jim Crow — I would feel it down to my core. I was not a crying child, except when I was being treated badly because of my race. In those instances — like when they wouldn't serve me at the drugstore counter in Raleigh — I would go home and sit on my bed and weep and weep and weep, the tears streaming down my face. *(Very upset.)* Now, Mama would come up and sit on the foot of my bed. She never said a word. She knew what I was feeling. She just did not want to encourage my rage. So my Mama would just sit and look at me while I cried, and it comforted me. I knew that she understood, and that was the most soothing salve. *(Sadie holds up a pair of crystal goblets.)*

SADIE.   These were Mama's too. Aren't they lovely? *(Bessie sets candlesticks and two serving dishes. Sadie finishes setting the gob-*

lets, sets a gravy boat and serving bowls.)
BESSIE. The words used to describe us most often were colored, Negro, black, and nigger. I've also been called jiggerboo, pickaninny, coon — you name it, honey. Some of these words are worse than others, and how mean they are depends on who is saying them and why. Personally, I don't use the word black very often to describe myself and my sister. To us, black was a person who was, well, black, and honey, I mean *black as your shoe.* I'm not black, I'm brown! Actually, the best word to describe me, I think, is colored. I am a colored woman or a Negro woman. Either one is OK. People dislike those words now. Today they use this term *African American.* It wouldn't occur to us to use that. We prefer to think of ourselves as Americans, that's all! *(Sadie gets large serving platter. Bessie sets serving spoons.)*
SADIE. There was an attitude among some Negroes that to be lighter-skinned was more desirable. But it was not something that was even *discussed* in our household. We were different shades, and it didn't make a bit of difference if you were white, black,
BESSIE and SADIE. *(Together.)* grizzly, or gray, you were you.
SADIE. Excuse me. *(Sadie exits to the kitchen with platter. Bessie reaches for the flower vase.)*
BESSIE. I think I'm just as good as anyone. That's the way I was brought up. I'll tell you a secret: I think I'm *better!* Ha! I remember being aware that colored people were supposed to feel inferior. I knew I was a smart little thing, a personality, an individual — a human being! I couldn't understand how people could look at me and not see that, because it sure was obvious to me. *(The stage revolves. Bessie enters the kitchen. Sadie is slicing vegetables.)*
SADIE. Now Mama and Papa tried to protect us when we were small, but we were quite young when we learned colored folks were being murdered. *(Bessie gives Sadie the vase.)*
BESSIE. They were being lynched. *(Sadie fills vase at the sink.)*
SADIE. Yes — we would hear the teachers talking among themselves about some poor Negro just walking down the side

of the road, in the wrong place, at the wrong time.

BESSIE. Those rebby boys would just grab him and hang him from a tree, just for fun.

SADIE. It was like entertainment to those fellas. *(Bessie cuts the flowers at the table. She arranges them in the vase.)*

BESSIE. The rebby boys would come in the middle of the night, and get him out of his bed and hang him up, in front of his wife and children. Sometimes they'd hang his whole family. Why, there was one story we heard of a pregnant colored woman who was hung from her feet, and they slit her abdomen open and let the fetus fall out —

SADIE. *(Quietly overlaps Bessie.)* Lord have mercy!

BESSIE. and she and her unborn baby just died right there, like that.

SADIE. I don't understand any of this.

BESSIE. It doesn't make any more sense to me now than it did then. If it weren't for those kind white missionaries at Saint Aug's, and my mother's white relatives who loved me, I would have hated all white people. Every last one. *(She looks at Sadie who shakes her head.)* Once in a while, God sends a good white person my way, even to this day. I think it's God's way of keeping me from becoming too mean. And when he sends a nice one to me, then I have to eat crow. And honey, crow is a tough old bird to eat, let me tell you. *(Bessie exits to dining room, sets flowers in the center of the table. Sadie continues to chop vegetables in the kitchen.)*

SADIE. I sometimes think maybe we were a little too sheltered. Why, I was almost afraid of men, really. I wasn't allowed to go downtown by myself until I was a grown girl and then I was always kind of jittery. You can imagine that when it came time for me to graduate from Saint Aug's, I didn't want to leave. The campus was the only home I'd ever known. But on graduation day, Papa said to me, "Daughter, you are college material. You owe it to your nation, your race, and yourself to go. And if you don't, then shame on you!" Well, it seemed to me that I had no choice but to go on with my schooling. *(Bessie reenters, puts on her apron.)* But Papa said to me, to both of us, "Daughters, I have no money, and you mustn't take a scholarship. If you take a scholarship, you will be beholden to the people who gave you the money. You must make your own way." So I started looking for teaching jobs and I found out there was an opening for being a supervisor, which involved visiting schools all over Wake County, North Carolina. Well, I had to learn to drive and I learned to drive Lemuel's car, and naturally, since I had learned to drive, Bessie decided she needed to learn, too. It seems to me she landed Lemuel's car in a ditch while she was learning!

BESSIE. I did no such thing! *(Sits.)*

SADIE. Lemuel wasn't too happy. *(Bessie scrapes carrots.)* I got to be a good driver, and when Mr. Booker T. Washington would come to visit Raleigh, he would climb into the passenger seat of Lemuel's car and I would drive him all around the county and show him my schools. He was so appreciative of the work I was doing.

BESSIE. When we were teaching, we saw for the first time what life was really like for our people.

SADIE. Yes, Lord.

BESSIE. It made our hearts bleed.

SADIE. I realized I was a child of privilege and I had to share my good fortune. I kept remembering what Papa always said: "Your mission ..."

BESSIE and SADIE. *(Together.)* "... is to help somebody."

SADIE. Yes, those words kept me going.

BESSIE. This was just forty-five years after the Surrender, and most of these Negroes were in bad shape, honey. They needed help with the basics.

SADIE. You see, oftentimes, learning to read and write for the children was not the top priority. Teaching people about food preparation — like how to can food — was more important.

BESSIE. A lot of the time what those folks needed was inspiration.

SADIE. Yes, a little encouragement. That goes a long way.

BESSIE. I remember when I left home to teach. I was twenty years old. I'd never been away from home. Papa took me to the train station in Raleigh and I put on a brave front. But

when that train pulled away from the station and I looked back and saw my Papa standing there, watching me, I thought I was going to die. I started to sob. I cried so hard that the people from the white car came to the colored car to get a look at this little darky just carrying on! Well, I'm embarrassed to say I created quite a commotion. The conductor came along and said, "What's the matter, did somebody die?" Now what'd he have to go and say that for? It was my girlhood that was dying and I knew it. *(Sadie crosses to Bessie at table.)*
SADIE.   Well it turned out you were the most exciting thing to happen to Boardman, North Carolina, in about a hundred years. Child, they'd never seen the likes of her! She'd walk through that town and the colored men would just stop and stare. They wouldn't say a word, they'd just take off their hats when she walked by.
BESSIE.   *(Laughs.)* One time, I turned and said, "Just what are you looking at?" They didn't answer. Finally, one of them said, "Why Miss Delany, we can't help it; you look just like a slice of Heaven." And I said, "Well, I ain't *your* slice of Heaven, so put your eyes back in yo' *head.*
SADIE.   Child, she meant business.
BESSIE.   Don't go thinking because Sadie and I are maiden ladies that we didn't have our share of beaus. We were popular, good-looking gals, but I think we were too smart, too independent for most men. *(Sadie begins to score cucumber. Bessie clears the carrots to the counter and exits to the dining room.)*
SADIE.   I had one beau named Frank — who was particularly fond of me. He was a fellow student of Lemuel's, studying medicine at Shaw University. Papa used to get kind of annoyed with Frank because he talked too much, and would keep talking even when Papa thought it was time for him to leave. So Papa would just clear his throat and stomp around, hoping Frank would get the hint.
BESSIE.   *(Opening the door.)* We had to almost shove Frank out the door!
SADIE.   I liked Frank a lot, but then one day, Papa told me, "Sadie, you won't be seeing any more of Frank for now." It seems Lemuel had reported to Papa that Frank had been

linked to some scandal, I never learned the details. All I know is that I never saw Frank again. Well, here I am an old maid. Oops, I shouldn't say "old maid" 'cause it makes Bessie mad.

BESSIE. *(Enters with a bag of potatoes.)* We are not old maids. We are maiden ladies.

SADIE. Well, whatever we are, I have no regrets about it. I think Frank would have worried me to death. I've had a good life, child. *(Sadie exits into dining room. Bessie puts six potatoes in a bowl.)*

BESSIE. I suppose Lemuel and Papa thought they were doing the right thing by Sadie, forbidding her to see Frank anymore, but I don't think it was right. She was a grown woman. It was her choice to make, not theirs! She should have had a say in the matter. Oh, I don't know what she saw in old Frank, anyway. He was kind of dull and talked too much, though I guess I shouldn't say that, because I can out-talk anyone. Yes, sir! I don't know how Sadie's put up with this old flabbermouth for the past one hundred years. *(Sadie reenters with a serving dish for the cucumber and passes a small photo to Bessie.)*

SADIE. I don't know how I have either! I found this picture of you teaching in Brunswick. Remember, it was on your way to your job in Brunswick — you came close to being lynched — *(Bessie looks at photo, puts it in her pocket, then starts to scrub potatoes.)*

BESSIE. Oh, yes ... that's right. I had to change trains in Waycross, Georgia. I was sitting in the little colored waiting room at the station, and I took my hair down and was combing it.

SADIE. She had hair down to *here.* *(She indicates her knee.)*

BESSIE. I was fixing myself up. I was going to my new job, and I wanted to look nice. There was no one in there except me and two colored teachers from New York who were traveling with me to Brunswick.

SADIE. So, there she was with her long hair down when this white man opened the door to the colored waiting room.

BESSIE. The white man stuck his head in and started, well, leering at me. He was drunk, and he smelled bad, and he started mumbling things. And I said, "Oh, why don't you shut

31

up and go wait with your own kind in the white waiting room?"

SADIE.   *(Overlapping.)* hmmmm ... hmmmmmmm ... hm ... hmmmmmmm ... hmmmmmmmm....

BESSIE.   He slammed the door and I could hear him shouting at the top of his lungs outside, "The nigger bitch insulted me! The nigger bitch insulted me!"

SADIE.   The two colored teachers slipped out the back and made a beeline for the woods.

BESSIE.   Yes! They hid in the woods! I guess I can't blame them. Well, I could see a crowd begin to gather on the platform, and I knew I was in big trouble.

SADIE.   Papa always said, "If you see a crowd, you go the other way."

BESSIE.   I was just waiting for somebody to get a rope. Thousands of Negroes had been lynched for far less than what I had just done. But I just continued to sit on the bench, combing my hair, while that white man was a-carrying on! You see, if you act real scared, sometimes that spurs them on. *(She gets to her feet.)* Two things saved me: that glorious, blessed train rounded the bend, breaking up the crowd and giving me my way to get on out of there. And it helped that the white man was drunk as a skunk, and that turned off some of the white people. But I wasn't afraid to die! I know you ain't got to die but once, and it seemed as good a reason to die as any. I was ready. Lord, help me, I was ready.

SADIE.   You were a *fool* to provoke that white man. You should have ignored him.

BESSIE.   How do you ignore some drunk, smelly white man treating you like trash?

SADIE.   Sometimes, it's better to put up with it, and live to tell about it. At the very least you should have run off into the woods with those other two teachers.

BESSIE.   *(To the audience.)* I told you: I would rather *die* than back down, honey ...

SADIE.   You are lucky to be alive. *(Quick fade to black as Sadie exits.)*

Harlem–Town

Images and music of 1900s and 1920s Harlem. The sisters place fresh pineapple and cherries on a ham. They work together in perfect synchronicity. Sadie looks up.

SADIE.   We made our first trip to New York City with our Mama in 1915.

BESSIE.   On that first visit, we could not get over the size of New York.

SADIE.   There were so many different *kinds* of people, from all over the world. In North Carolina, there were white people, Negroes, and Indians. That was it.

BESSIE.   In New York, there were Irish people, German people, Jewish people, Italian people, and so on. So many different kinds of white people!

SADIE.   And they ate different foods and you could smell strange things cooking ...

BESSIE.   And you'd hear voices, speaking different languages ...

SADIE.   We stayed with friends of the family for a few days, then we went home. But we wanted more!

BESSIE.   So when we returned to Raleigh, we talked to Papa about moving to New York to attend college.

SADIE.   By then we were grown women, twenty-four and twenty-six years old, and toughened up by our rural teaching years.

BESSIE.   So when a Presbyterian minister asked Mama, "Aren't y'all afraid to let those girls go up to Harlem-town?"

SADIE.   Mama said: "No, I'm not afraid to let my girls go anywhere. We've taught them right from wrong and if they don't do what's right, there's nothing we can do about it now." *(Sadie puts cherries in refrigerator.)*

BESSIE.   Eventually, all of us Delany children, except Lemuel, moved to New York City.

SADIE.   Our brother, Lucius, was the first one of us to get an apartment and he let us all move in with him — *(Sadie picks up the ham to put in oven.)*

BESSIE.   in a three-room apartment at 2505

BESSIE and SADIE.   *(Together.)* Seventh Ave.

BESSIE.   at the corner of 145th Street.

SADIE.   Our share of the rent was nine dollars each. *(Bessie puts pineapple in refrigerator and takes out chicken. Sadie brings celery and butter to the table.)*

BESSIE.   I had always dreamed I would become a medical doctor, but I ran out of time and money. My brother, Hap, who was a dentist, tried to get me to enroll at New York University, where he had graduated. But this was 1918, and New York University would not take women in its dentistry program in 1918. *(Sadie gets stuffing from refrigerator.)*

SADIE.   So, she enrolled at Columbia University.

BESSIE.   Out of a class of about 170, there were 11 women, six colored men, and me. I was the *only colored woman!* It was the same for Sadie at Pratt Institute. *(Bessie washes chicken in sink.)* You know, I studied very hard in dentistry school, but I'd dissect a cadaver any day, rather than have to deal with some of those old white professors. Yes sir! To be fair — oh, it's so hard to be fair — I have to admit that some of them treated me just fine, but one instructor really had it in for me. There was an assignment where he failed me, yet I knew my work was good. One of my white girl friends,

BESSIE and SADIE.   *(Together.)* Sadie Goodman,

BESSIE.   the youngest one in the class — she said, "Bessie, let me turn in your work as if it was mine, and see what grade he gives it." I'll tell you what happened, honey. She passed with my failed work! That was the kind of thing that could make you crazy, as a Negro. It's no wonder some of us have stopped trying altogether. There are plenty of white folks who say "Why haven't Negroes gotten further than they have? What's wrong with them?" To those white people, I have this to say: *"Are you kidding?"* *(Bessie brings chicken to Sadie.)*

SADIE.   See, when you are colored, everyone is always looking for your faults. If you are going to make it, you have to be entirely honest, clean, brilliant, and so on. Because if you slip up once, the white folks say to each other,

BESSIE and SADIE. *(Together.)* "See, what'd I tell you."

SADIE. So you don't have to be as good as white people, you have to be *better or the best.*

BESSIE. When Negroes are average, *they fail,* unless they are very, very lucky. Now, if you're average and *white,* honey, you can go far. Just look at Dan Quayle. If that boy was colored he'd be washing dishes somewhere. *(Sadie stuffs chicken.)*

SADIE. I'll tell you a story. I got my first teaching job in New York in the fall of 1920. It was at P.S. 119 in Harlem, which was an elementary school, mostly colored. This was a typical assignment for a colored teacher. But I wanted to teach at a high school because it was a promotion and it paid better. So I had to be a little clever — Bessie would say

BESSIE. sneaky — *(Bessie stirs macaroni on stove.)*

SADIE. clever! to find ways to get around these brick walls they set up for colored folks. So I asked around quietly for some advice. A friend of my brother Hubert's, who worked for the Board of Education ...

BESSIE. ... he was colored ...

SADIE. Yes ... suggested a plan which I followed: I applied for a high school position, and when I reached the top of the list, I received a letter in the mail saying they wished to meet with me in person. Hubert's friend said:

BESSIE. "Skip the appointment."

SADIE. Yes. "Send them a letter," he said, "act like there's a mix-up. Then just show up on the first day of classes." Child, when I showed up that day — at Theodore Roosevelt High School, a white high school — they just about died when they saw me. A colored woman! But my name was on the list to teach there, and it was too late for them to send me someplace else. The plan had worked! I became the first colored teacher in the New York City system to teach domestic science on the high school level. I spent the rest of my career teaching at excellent high schools. I never let prejudice stop me from what I wanted to do in this life, child. Life is short, and it's up to you to make it sweet. *(Sadie puts chicken in the oven, gets cheese and a casserole dish. Bessie drains the macaroni.)*

BESSIE.   I was known in the Harlem community as "Dr. Bessie" to distinguish me from my brother Hap, who was known as "Dr. Delany." There was a time, in the 1920s, '30s, and '40s when just about every living soul in Harlem knew of Dr. Bessie. My patients would go on vacation and send postcards addressed only to "Dr. Bessie, New York City" and I would get those cards. This was the center of Harlem! From my office window you could see everything that was going on. Harlem was like a beehive, with people running every which way, going to work, school, church or to entertainment. It was a positive place in those days.

SADIE.   Now, being good girls, Bessie and I did not venture too far into the jazz scene. After all, we were Bishop Delany's daughters.

BESSIE.   That's right! We didn't want to have anything to do with smooth-talking men and their fast women. *(They begin to make the macaroni and cheese together.)*

SADIE.   If we went to a nightclub, it was always with a proper escort.

BESSIE.   Usually, we went to places like Ed Small's.

SADIE.   Our brother, Hubert, became friendly with many famous entertainers like

BESSIE.   Ethel Waters, Alberta Hunter ...

SADIE.   Oh, that Alberta Hunter was one of the nicest women we ever met.

BESSIE.   Fletcher Henderson, Cab Calloway ...

SADIE.   Duke Ellington ...

BESSIE.   ... and Lena Horne. James Weldon Johnson, the poet, was one of my patients.

SADIE.   We were acquainted with these people, but our close friends were in the professional set. Like Mr. William Kelly, the editor of the *Amsterdam News* — he never passed up an invitation for our cooking. *(They laugh. When Sadie isn't looking, Bessie slathers lots of butter on top of the macaroni and cheese. Sadie taps her hand.)* You're a naughty old gal.

BESSIE.   I use butter when no one's looking! *(Sadie covers macaroni and cheese and tidies up. Bessie crosses to refrigerator for a glass of water, then sits.*) When I started my practice in Harlem in 1923, I charged two dollars for a cleaning, two dollars for an extraction, five dollars for a silver filling, and ten dollars for a gold filling. What was I charging when I retired? The same thing, of course! I never raised my rates because I was getting by OK. *(Sadie starts to make gravy.)*

SADIE. In the '20s, Bessie's office became a meeting place for Negro activists in Harlem. *(To Bessie.)* Remember the time you got Frazier and his friends to protest —

BESSIE. *(Indicating the gravy.)* I'll do that!

SADIE. No, you *will not!* You burn my pans. You do it all the time. They get black on the bottom.

BESSIE. I don't! If you'd just let me do it my way. *(To the audience:)* I have a wrought iron pan. I like to cook *everything* in *that pan. Everything.* Just like our grandpa, Mr. Miliam, taught us the old fashion way. *(To Sadie.)* I never burned *that* pan!

SADIE. And you won't burn another one of mine either! Now go on and tell them about Frazier. *(Bessie won't. So Sadie does.)* E. Franklin Frazier was a graduate student at Columbia with me when I was getting my Masters in Education there. *(Sadie looks at Bessie. She doesn't respond.)* He was a great friend of ours.

BESSIE. Anyway! One time I got tired of listening to Frazier and his friends planning another sit in. *(Sadie goes back to her gravy.)* They had just re-released the film *Birth of a Nation,* a very mean-spirited film which degraded Negroes. It was showing at the Capitol Theater in Manhattan. This was in about what — 1925?

SADIE. Yes, 1925.

BESSIE. So I said to Frazier, "How can y'all sit around here planning those silly sit-ins when they're showing *Birth of a Nation* at the Capitol? I don't know about you, but I'm going down there tonight and protest. And if you don't join me, well, shame on you!" Well, I guess I inspired them. But what happened is kind of funny —

SADIE. — at least to you. *(Sadie gets garnish for ham, and places ham on dish with garnish.)*

BESSIE. Hap had a patient with an emergency and I stayed to help, so we were late. Well, we got there just in time to see the cops throwing poor Frazier, W.E.B. Du Bois and Walter White into the police wagon. The next day, those boys chewed me out good! They came to my office and said, "You convinced us to protest and then you didn't show up! You have a lot of nerve!" And I said, "Well, Hap and I did show up, it's just that y'all were too busy getting yourselves arrested to notice." They didn't think it was too funny.

SADIE. But all you had to do was say the word "protest" and Bessie was usually there! She marched in more protests in New York City than anyone cares to remember. I never did like protests. No, no, no, I do not like confrontations.

BESSIE. There were a lot of colored people like Sadie. Really, those were the two extremes. On the one hand you had Booker T. Washington, a smoother of the waters, not a radical.

SADIE. He's not appreciated today, but he did a lot for our people getting them educated. He wanted you to be literate, to own your forty acres and a mule.

BESSIE. Sadie is more like Booker T. Washington. *(Sadie sits with Bessie at the table.)*

SADIE. And on the other hand, you had W.E.B. Du Bois, a militant. More like Bessie.

BESSIE. I can still see his face: he was a good-looking, brown-skinned man with a mustache, and very intelligent-looking eyes. Dr. Du Bois was the editor of *The Crisis* and was always speaking out against one thing or another —

SADIE. Many people thought his approach was too fast,

BESSIE. too threatening to white people

SADIE. and therefore dangerous for Negroes. Now, Dr. Du Bois knew our Papa because at that time, there were very, very few educated, prominent Negroes. He never stayed with Papa when he came to visit in Raleigh.

BESSIE. He stayed with Lemuel.

SADIE. Papa was not aggressive enough by Dr. Du Bois's standards.

38

BESSIE.   Still, I believe in Dr. Du Bois's approach: I would have given life and limb to the cause.

SADIE.   Sometimes, colored women were not even welcome in the movement, Bessie.

BESSIE.   Too bad, I was there whether they liked it or not!

SADIE.   *(She laughs.)* That's true!

BESSIE.   I was torn between two issues — colored, and women's rights. It seemed to me that no matter how much I had to put up with as a woman, the bigger problem was being colored.

SADIE.   That's right.

BESSIE.   Though one of the happiest days of my life was back in 1920,

BESSIE and SADIE.   *(Together.)* when women got the right to vote.

BESSIE.   Sadie and I registered to vote immediately and we have never missed a chance to vote since.

SADIE.   Now, where we vote, the people at the polls have come to know us. They say, "Here come the Delany sisters. We knew you'd get here,

BESSIE and SADIE.   *(Together.)* one way or another!"

BESSIE.   Of course we'd get there! Negroes, more than anyone, need to make sure they vote, to make themselves heard in the system.

SADIE.   We've come a long, long way in a short, short time since slavery days, and there's no use in quitting now.

BESSIE.   It's true that you can't change the world with your one vote, but if you don't vote, you don't have the right to complain. And honey, I surely do not want to give up my right to complain, no, sir!

Blackout

END ACT TWO

ACT THREE

Ties That Bind

Lights come up on the Delany sisters in the kitchen listening to the hymn Lift Every Voice.* *They are peeling oranges. After an interval:*

SADIE.   *(Turning radio off.)* That was Papa's favorite hymn.

BESSIE.   In April 1928, Lemuel sent a telegram, "Come home quick, Papa's very ill." I did not get to Raleigh in time to see him. He had died, peacefully, at home. I saw his body. He had beautiful hands, and when I saw those hands I realized it was true, that he was gone from this Earth. All our brothers came, and for a long time, people remembered how those six Delany sons — three on each side — carried Papa's coffin to the chapel. They were tall, good-looking boys and it was quite a sight, the way they lifted Papa's coffin up on their shoulders. Poor Mama was mourning and grieving like the world was coming to an end. I remember telling her — she was a good-looking woman even then — that it would be OK by me if she wanted to remarry someday.

SADIE.   Mama said, "I've had my husband, and I don't want another one, 'cause there's no one else that can compare."

BESSIE.   I stayed behind in Raleigh to help Mama pack her things, which was very hard.

SADIE.   She had so many belongings and memories to let go of. *(Sadie gets bowl of sugar.)* Papa's death hit me hard. I didn't realize how safe I felt in this world because of Papa. Even after I moved to New York, I knew that somehow he was watching out for me. But even as a grown woman, forty years

---

* See Special Note on Songs and Recordings on copyright page.

old or more, I was still something of a mama's child. I loved to be in the company of my Mama and I would just do anything for her. *(They start to cut oranges.)*

BESSIE.   While Papa was still alive, Mama had never seen much of the world at all.

SADIE.   She had the whole world on her shoulders as the bishop's wife and being the matron at Saint Aug's.

BESSIE.   So after we moved her up to New York, she was ready to go places.

SADIE.   Even when she was very elderly, all you had to do was say, "Let's go," and she'd say,

BESSIE and SADIE.   *(Together.)* "Just let me get my hat."

BESSIE.   Some of the happiest days of Sadie's life were going on trips with Mama — especially when they went abroad in the summer of 1930.

SADIE.   The most memorable moment of the trip came in London, when we went to see Paul Robeson in *Othello.* Paul's performance in the play was legendary, because he interpreted Othello from the perspective of a Negro man, which was a very important breakthrough in the history of theater. When Paul heard Mama and I were there, he was ecstatic. He had us brought backstage right away. He said it was so good to see some Delanys from Harlem! But he seemed a little homesick.

BESSIE.   Paul Robeson was not treated well in his later years. *(Bessie gets up to discard orange peels.)* Sadie and I were in charge of Mama's happiness, but I think Hubert gave Mama her greatest moment as an old lady.

SADIE.   Oh, he certainly did! You know, there wasn't a soul in Harlem who didn't know our brother Hubert. He was very active in the NAACP, an assistant U.S. attorney —

BESSIE.   He prosecuted five hundred cases and lost only two! Where's his picture?

SADIE.   There! There! Over there!

BESSIE.   Now, Hubert had been the attorney and adviser for the singer Marian Anderson —

SADIE.   That was back in 1939 when the Daughters of the American Revolution kept her from singing in Constitution Hall in Washington

BESSIE.   because she was colored.

SADIE.   And then Mrs. Roosevelt intervened and arranged for Marian to sing at the Lincoln Memorial.

BESSIE.   Oh, that Mrs. Roosevelt was ahead of her time about equality of the races. To this day, we admire Eleanor Roosevelt more than any other famous white person.

SADIE.   So, as a surprise for Mama, Hubert arranged for her to *meet* Eleanor Roosevelt!

BESSIE.   When we came into the room, there she was, and she jumped up like a jackrabbit to greet Mama, taking her hand. It was pretty wonderful to see the former First Lady of the United States jump up, so respectful-like, to greet Mama, an old colored lady. *(Sadie gets grater for coconut.)* You know, our Mama — and Sadie, too — could cook a meal for almost nothing. You never saw people who could live cheaper than we could. In fact, you remember! we *fed* people during the Depression.

SADIE.   Well, of course we did! *(Sadie gets coconut from refrigerator and starts to grate the coconut.)*

BESSIE.   I remember when that old stock market crashed, rich white men were jumping out of buildings and things like that. I can't imagine having so little faith in the Lord, and so much faith in money, that you would end your life over a little thing like losing your fortune. The Lord says money is Evil, and He is right! Money is the root of every mess you can think of, including slavery. Greed! Profiting off the backs of others!

SADIE.   Now Bessie kept her practice going during the Depression, although now I wonder how you did.

BESSIE.   Remember the day, one of my patients went to sign up for help from the government —

SADIE.   Oh, yes.

BESSIE.   and she asked me to go along to keep her company?

SADIE.   They gave her some kind of little job.

BESSIE.   And I wasn't planning on this at all, but I said, "Say, do you have anything for me? I am a licensed dentist and I'm not doing so well myself." Well, next thing I knew, the government set up a clinic near City Hall, with me running it, but it wasn't no handout, no, sir! Let me make that perfectly clear. It was work-for-hire. I have never taken a handout from the government in my life. I am the kind of Negro that most white people don't know about. Or maybe they don't want to know about. Just listen to that fella, David Duke, down in Louisiana — the fella that was with the Klan and then he was going to run for president. David Duke doesn't think there are Negroes like me and Sadie, colored folks who have never done nothin' except *contribute* to America. Well, we are just as good Americans as he is — better! Yes, I think I'm going to write a letter, and I'm going to say, "Dear Mr. Duke: This is just to set the record straight. I am a Negro woman. I was brought up in a good family. My Papa was a devoted father. I went to college; I paid my own way. I am not stupid. I'm not on welfare. And I'm not scrubbing floors. Especially not yours." *(Bessie exits.)*

SADIE.   By the 1930s we had a heap of nieces and nephews and we loved them all dearly. But one of them, Little Hubie, had a special place in our hearts. He was damaged when he was born. He was what we called a spastic child. Little Hubie couldn't walk, so Julia pushed him around in a carriage. *(Bessie enters with the ambrosia dish and gives it to Sadie as she is talking. Bessie sits.)* Little Hubie had a very active mind. His cousin, Harry, who was the same age as Little Hubie, was a very bright little boy, but one time we were giving Harry a spelling lesson and he spelled a word incorrectly. Little Hubie was sitting nearby and he banged his hand on the table and shook his head.

BESSIE.   He knew that Harry had spelt it wrong! *(They begin making the ambrosia, layering the oranges and fresh coconut. After each layer Bessie sprinkles sugar.)*

SADIE.   Dean, Bessie's boyfriend at the time was there that day and he was particularly fond of Little Hubie. So one day Bessie asked him, "You think Little Hubie is going to be all right, don't you Dean?" She was really looking for him to agree with her, you know. But he didn't answer. She asked again. "You think Little Hubie is going to be all right, don't you?" And he finally said, "No, Bessie, I do not." It had just never occurred to us that Little Hubie would die.

BESSIE. We just thought that with enough prayer, enough love, and enough determination we would overcome this. But it wasn't part of God's plan.

SADIE. It was pneumonia that finally took him from us. He was ten years old when he died. It was during the war, the date was the seventh of March, 1943. Bessie still sleeps with his blanket on her bed. Little Hubie's death humbled us. We were sort of cocky before that. We thought we could do anything, fix any problem. We were not afraid of adversity. We were Delanys! After Little Hubie, we realized you can't always get what you want in life. *(Sadie clears the cutting boards and coconut plate to the sink. A beat.)*

BESSIE. After the war was over, we bought a little cottage in the North Bronx with a garden. It was like the country. The first thing we did was to hire a man to put a porch on. Remember? He laughed at us.

SADIE. He said, "You're going to put a porch on that little old two-room cottage?"

BESSIE. And we were very annoyed at him. We said, "Mister, we're from North Carolina and we've been cooped up in apartments since the

BESSIE and SADIE. *(Together.)* First World War.

BESSIE. Now we've got this house out in the country, and where we're from, a house ain't a home

BESSIE and SADIE. *(Together.)* unless it's got itself a porch!"

BESSIE. So we got ourselves a porch. *(Sadie brings a bowl of butter to the table and begins to cream the butter. Bessie measures the dry ingredients.)*

SADIE. Mama was getting very elderly, getting on ninety years old, and we wanted her to live forever. When the weather was nice, we would each take her by the arm, on either side, and we would walk around the neighborhood.

BESSIE. One little boy yelled at us, "Look, *three* grandmas going for a walk." We thought it was funny. But it was true, we were getting old, too. *(They laugh.)*

SADIE. And soon, we started having trouble keeping Mama in line.

BESSIE.   Something Mama would do, she would give money to strangers —

SADIE.   just like when we were children and Uncle Jesse and all the hoboes would come by and she would always fix them a plate of food.

BESSIE.   It got so bad that we would rush home from our jobs every day in fear.

SADIE.   Finally, we decided that one of us was going to have to quit working and take care of Mama. What else could we do?

BESSIE.   Well, it was obvious that I was the one who should quit my job, even though Sadie was the mama's child.

SADIE.   If I continued working until 1960, I would get $150 a month pension from the New York City Board of Education, and split three ways, living together, we could manage on that. *(Bessie brings the dry ingredients to Sadie.)*

BESSIE.   And I was a dentist, working independently, and had no pension plan. So it was settled. I was to close my practice. I was only fifty-nine years old and I had planned to work for many years yet. But once the decision was made, I accepted it. *(Bessie sits.)* Mama had been a perfect housekeeper and I thought that's what she wanted. She would say, "Bessie, why don't you just sit down here next to me?" And I would say, "In a minute, Mama, when I'm done shaking out the rugs," or whatever. But she didn't want brass fixtures that gleamed like gold; she wanted *me*. She was an old lady and she wanted her child to just sit with her, to be near her. Now that I am very old I understand this. *(To Sadie.)* Why didn't I just spend more time with Mama? *(Sadie comforts her, pats her hand. Bessie gets up and crosses to the counter.)* But hard times were coming. First, Manross died of a heart attack on November 3, 1955. When it happened, I called Lemuel on the telephone and I said, *(Cracking eggs into a bowl.)* "Lemuel, sit down, I have some bad news." He said, "OK, I'm ready. It's Mama, isn't it?" I said, "No, it's Manross." He just said, "Manross? Manross? Manross?"

SADIE.   Losing Manross was a shock to all of us. He was the first of our generation to die, and we knew there would be more dying because we Delanys tend to die in threes.

BESSIE.   Strange thing is, it was Lemuel who went to Glory next.

SADIE.   He died of a heart attack two months later. Coming so close onto Manross's death, this was a terrible blow to poor Mama. *(Bessie gives Sadie the beaten eggs.)*

BESSIE.   She hadn't gotten over Manross yet, and I had to sit her down and tell her about Lemuel, and she cried and cried. *(Sadie folds eggs into cake mix. Bessie sits, pours in vanilla and almond extract.)*

SADIE.   She wasn't just sad, she was kind of angry. I don't think she ever expected to out-live any of her children.

BESSIE.   After she lost Manross and Lemuel, I guess it was only natural that Mama was ready to go. But to tell you what a silly old gal I am, I have to admit I did not realize when Mama was leaving us. I did not realize my Mama was dying. The day it happened Mama had been ailing and stayed in bed. Sadie was sitting at the head of the bed, and I was just kind of hovering around. Silly me, I left the room. It was getting dark and I wanted to feed my pet dogs and birds. Then Sadie came outside and said, "Bess, Mama's gone." Bad as it was for me, Mama's death was ten times worse for Sadie. Sweet sister Sadie just cried for weeks and weeks. Every time we sat down for a meal, with Mama's chair sitting there empty, the tears would come streaming down Sadie's face. Why, I wasn't sure she would make it. *(Bessie gets up. She takes the bowls to the sink.)* I'll tell you something kind of funny. It had annoyed Mama that when Manross died, they made his wife return the pension check he had in his pocket. Mama thought that was mean. So she said to Sadie, "If I die and I have a check in my pocket, you must promise me that you will run to the bank and cash it, and keep that money!" So, while Mama was ailing, Sadie did just that. And do you know that the pension company sent a letter immediately? They had seen Mama's obituary in *The New York Times* — that Bishop Delany's widow had died — and they sent a letter that said, "Please return the last check." And Sadie wrote to them, "Sorry, but it was cashed." We *always* did what Mama asked. *(Bessie exits with a dessert tray. Sadie continues to stir batter, stops.)*

SADIE. Now, you might ask, what happens to a mama's child when her Mama passes on? Well, it was worse than anything. Her passing hurt me something terrible. I was so dependent on my Mama. When I was a grown woman and moved up to New York, I wrote at least one letter every day to my Mama, back in North Carolina. Child, a day didn't go by that I didn't send her a letter, or sometimes two. And after Papa died, and Mama left Raleigh and moved in with me and Bessie, I was so glad. Until the day she died, Mama called me her "shadow." So when she died I thought, Maybe I should die myself. *(She breaks down.)* I was depressed. *(She gets up.)* But Mama was gone, and I had to think about the world in a completely different way. Bessie says that for the first time in my life, I seemed to come into my own, as an individual person. I was sixty-seven years old. *(Bessie enters. Sadie crosses to the counter to grease a cake pan.)* Since our eldest brother Lemuel had died, and Papa had died long before, Mama's passing meant I was now the head of the family. There was never a family decision that didn't get brought to me for my opinion. This was hard on Bessie. It was easy for her to let Mama be the boss, but it was hard for her to play second fiddle to me.

BESSIE. You're older than I am, so whatever you decide goes.

SADIE. I think it about kills you to say that, *(Bessie laughs.)* but she does abide by it. Now, one day, Bessie went to visit our brother Hap at his home in Mount Vernon, in the suburbs. While she was there, Hap's wife put this idea in Bessie's head that maybe the two of us ought to get out of the Bronx and move into their neighborhood in Westchester. *(They pour batter into cake pan.)*

BESSIE. I didn't think we could afford it, but then I sat down and figured out we *could.*

SADIE. Bessie says now that she had an ulterior motive in moving us out of the Bronx. She says she didn't think I would ever get over Mama's death, and that maybe by moving away and starting over, it would help. I think she was right. *(Lights fade as Sadie moves to put the cake in the oven.)*

Outliving The Rebby Boys

Images of the 50s and early 60s civil rights demonstrations: Rosa Parks, the integration of Little Rock, Dr. King's march from Selma to Montgomery. More images as lights reveal the Delany sisters in the sitting room. It is approaching evening. Bessie places Sadie's shawl around her shoulders. Sadie helps Bessie put on her jacket. As they finish, the images dissolve and lights go up.

SADIE. Today, all of Mount Vernon, it seems, is mostly Negro, but in 1957, it was mostly white.

BESSIE. I don't think either Sadie or I had ever lived among so many white folks before, and it was a bit of a shock to us. Of course, we were a bit of a shock to *them.*

SADIE. Our brother Hap had broken the neighborhood; he was the first colored person to move in here.

BESSIE. They wouldn't let him buy a house.

SADIE. So do you know what Hap did?

BESSIE. He *built* a house.

SADIE. He just went and bought a piece of land right smack in the middle of the nicest white neighborhood, and before the neighbors could figure out what was happening, they were pouring the foundation.

BESSIE. The first time I answered the door at our house in Mount Vernon, it was some white lady from Welcome Wagon and she went on and on about this and that and then she said to me:

SADIE. "And be sure you tell the owner ..."

BESSIE. And I said, "Lady, I have news for you. I *am* the owner." Well, she just about dropped dead. It was clear she thought I was the *maid.*

SADIE. You know — it was during that time, during the civil rights movement when we thought: Maybe now it will finally happen.

BESSIE. Maybe now our country will finally grow up, come

to terms with this race mess.

SADIE. But it seems like the momentum was lost when the Vietnam War happened.

BESSIE. It was like all the energy of the young people, and the focus of the country, got shifted away from civil rights.

SADIE. But it wasn't just Vietnam that slowed down the progress we made in the civil rights movement —

BESSIE. It had a lot to do with lack of leadership after Martin Luther King died.

SADIE. As far as Bessie and I are concerned, Martin Luther King was an *angel!*

BESSIE. He just dropped from Heaven.

SADIE. And there hasn't been anyone as special since then.

BESSIE. Now, I know that Martin Luther King was not perfect. There are all these stories coming out about him now; they may not be true at all.

SADIE. And if they are? We never expected him to be perfect.

BESSIE. He was a man, after all. I didn't expect him to be Jesus Christ.

SADIE. Yes. Things have kind of slid downhill as far as equality is concerned.

BESSIE. And the 1980s were the worst yet, yes, sir! Sadie and I are registered Independents, but we usually favor the Democrats.

SADIE. We loved Jimmy Carter because he was an honest man, and his heart was in the right place.

BESSIE. And I liked Harry Truman.

SADIE. You surely liked that "Buck Stops Here" business.

BESSIE. I'll tell you something, honey: I would have made a very good president. That's right! *Me!* I would have done well. I'm honest and I'm tough and I could get the job done, yes, sir! If I was president, the first thing I would do would be to say that people over one hundred years of age no longer have to pay taxes! Ha ha! Lord knows I've paid my share. But I guess it will be a thousand years — probably never — before a colored person is elected president of the United States.

SADIE. There will be a Negro President someday ...

BESSIE. No, no. I think white people would rather die than have a Negro president. I predict there will be a white woman president before there is a Negro president. And if a Negro is elected president? That person will be a Negro *woman*.

SADIE. How do you know that?

BESSIE. I'm a little psychic. Like with that Clarence Thomas mess, the Supreme Court nomination. He's lying. That girl, Anita Hill, was telling the *truth*. And Sadie says, "How do you know that?" And I say, I know a rascal when I see one! *(Beat.)* You know, Sadie has taken on this business of getting old like it's a big *project*.

SADIE. Yes. I started doing yoga exercises about forty years ago. Well, when Bessie turned eighty she decided that I looked better than her. So she decided she would start doing yoga, too. And we've been doing our exercises together ever since. But, sometimes, Bessie cheats. I'll be doing an exercise and look over at her, and she's just lying there! Bessie is a naughty old gal.

BESSIE. I try to be good. Every morning, after we do our yoga, we each take a clove of garlic …

SADIE. Chop it up, and swallow it whole so there's no odor.

BESSIE. We also take a teaspoon of cod liver oil. I think it's disgusting.

SADIE. We eat as many as seven different vegetables a day. Plus lots of fresh fruits. And we take vitamins and minerals. And I make Bessie take tyrosine when she's a little blue.

BESSIE. We eat our big meal of the day at noon. In the evening, we usually have a milk shake for dinner, and then we go upstairs and watch *MacNeil Lehrer* on the TV.

SADIE. After that, we say our prayers. We say prayers in the morning and before we go to bed. It takes a long time to pray for everyone, because it's a big family and tonight —

BESSIE and SADIE. *(Together.)* we are going to pray for *you*.

BESSIE. Truth is, we've gotten so old Sadie's starting to get a little *bold*. Not long ago, some young men started hanging out in front of our house. They were part of a gang from the Bronx, and they just thought our dead-end street here was a good spot to play basketball and do drugs and I don't know what-all.

SADIE. Yes.... Well, Bessie said to me, "I'll go out there and get rid of them." And I said, "No, Bess. For once, I'm going to handle it. You stay in the house." *(Gets up from her chair.)* So I went on out there and said, "You boys better get out of here." They were kind of surprised. And then one of them said, "You can't make us leave. This is a public street." And I said, "Yes, it's a public street, but it's not a *park*, so get moving." And this fella said to me: "Just how do you think you're going to make us go?" I pointed to my house. I said, "My sister is inside and she has her hand on the phone to call the police." Of course, this was a little white lie because we don't have a phone, but they didn't know that. So the leader of this group laughed at me and he said, "You think the police are gonna come when some old woman calls them?" I said, "Yes, they will come. Because I own this property here, and I own this house, and I pay my taxes. They *will* come, and they will boot you on out of here." Well, *they left.* Bessie was kind of surprised that I took that gang on like that. To tell you the truth, so was I. *(Sadie sits.)*

BESSIE. Our Grandpa Miliam surely would have been proud of you. *(Sadie laughs.)* I was just thinking about Mr. Miliam this morning. There was a cute little squirrel in the yard, and I said, "Oh, you better be glad Mr. Miliam and his gun ain't around. 'Cause he'd shoot you and fry you up for his breakfast."

SADIE. I wonder what Mr. Miliam would think of his granddaughters living this long.

BESSIE. I think he'd get a kick out of it. I know he'd have lived longer if Grandma hadn't died and it broke his heart.

SADIE. Sometimes you need a reason to keep living.

BESSIE. I wouldn't be here without you. *(Sadie goes to her, holds her.)* I get the blues sometimes. It's a shock to me to be this old. Sometimes it hits me right between the eyes. I wake up and say "Oh, Lord, how did this happen?" Turning one hundred was the worst birthday of my life. I wouldn't wish it on my worst enemy. Turning 101 was not so bad. *(Sadie pats Bessie's shoulders, goes back to her chair.)* Once you're past that century mark, it's just not as shocking.

SADIE.   Longevity runs in the family. I'm sure that's part of why we're still here. As a matter of fact, until recently there were still five of us, of the original ten children.

BESSIE.   When good ol' Hap knew he was going to Glory, he was content. He was 95 years old. He said, "I've had a good life. I've done everything I wanted to do, I think I've done right by people."

SADIE.   We Delanys can usually say that, when our time comes.

BESSIE.   *(After a beat.)* Sadie! You know what I've been thinking lately? All those people who were mean to us in our lives ...

SADIE.   All those rebby boys —

BESSIE.   Why, they've turned to dust, and here we are —

BESSIE and SADIE.   *(Together.) Still here!*

BESSIE.   We've outlived the rebby boys!

SADIE.   Yes, that's one way to beat them! That's justice!

BESSIE.   They're turning in their graves, while me and sweet sister Sadie are getting the last word.

SADIE.   And you surely do love getting the last word.

BESSIE.   We're having our say, giving our opinion.

SADIE.   Lord ain't it good to be an *American.*

BESSIE.   I'll tell you a little secret: I'm starting to feel optimistic. *Maybe I'll get into Heaven after all.* I do have some redeeming qualities. I may have to hang on to Sadie's heels, but I'll get there.

SADIE.   *(She stands, crosses to us.)* You know, it has been a pleasure speaking with you. Why, I feel like I've known you all my life. And that's the truth. Won't you stay tonight and celebrate Papa's birthday with us? You *will?*

BESSIE and SADIE.   *(Together.)* How *wonderful* ... *(Bessie rises to join Sadie as lights fade.)*

END OF PLAY

PROPERTY PRE-SET LIST

ON STAGE

Dining table	SL
tea tray with sugar bowl, spoon, creamer	On DR corner of table
2 cups, 2 saucers with spoons	SL of tea tray on table
tray with:	
pitcher of water covered with napkin	Center of table
4 water glasses	Upside down on tray
2 napkins pressed flat and folded in half	US of tea tray
Six matching upholstered dining chairs	Around table
Sideboard	
6 water goblets	
6 wine glasses	
10 dinner plates-6 used	
large serving platter — behind tea cups	
gravy boat/plate	
small rectangular dish	
small oval plate	
small octangular bowl	
large oval serving dish	
2 candles	
2 candlesticks	
6 silver forks, spoons, knives	In silverware drawer SR
4 silver serving spoons	In silverware drawer SL
6 napkins	In linen drawer, CTR
6 placemats	On top of napkins
Flower vase	In SL lower cupboard

Additional sideboard <u>dressing</u> includes:
    1 sm. glass lamp with shade (practical)
    2 tea cups and saucers
    3 soup bowls
    7 small plates
    large serving dish with lid
    3 large serving platters on stands on top shelf
            (referred to as "mama's wedding pieces")
    rectangular deep dish with handles
    1 pie server in silverware drawer

Small round table with square table cloth	DC
large Bible with inscription	On table, SR
1 short-backed arm chair	SR of table
1 tall-backed arm chair	SR of table
Low bookcase	Against wall USR
3 photo albums	

#1 black photo album
    (papa)
    (Eliza & Mama)
	On top-SR side of
	    bookcase

#2 flower fabric album
    (mama & cooking class)
    (Sam in front of house)
    (Prof. Boyer teaching Sadie)
    (family picture circa 1896)
	On top–SL side of
	    bookcase

#3 black photo album/Jim Crow
    (J.C.)
    (lynching photo)
    (family photo with 'baby' Sam)
	Under #2 album on
	    bookcase

8 family photos displayed on shelf	On bookshelf SL
include:	
large family photo with 'baby' Sam	Sadie picks up to show audience

Additional bookcase/living room <u>dressing</u> includes:

large crystal vase	CL
1 crystal bowl	SR
misc. books	Bottom
3-4 books between bookends	On bookcase SL
small glass lamp with shade	On bookcase
floor lamp (practical)	SL of bookcase
trash can	On floor SR of bookcase

OFFSTAGE PRESETS: ACT ONE

Teapot with hot tea	Breakfast UL
Pot holder	Behind calendar on shelf
Paper cup with water for actor	On breakfront shelf
Two boxes of photos:	
#1: gray cardboard box with framed photos	On UL kitchen chair under #2 box
grandparents (hinged separate frame)	
Jordan Motley	
Eliza Logan	
Mama	
Martha Logan	
James Miliam	
Lemuel (in corner of box)	
#2: tan box with misc. unframed photos	On UL kitchen chair on top #1 box

ACT TWO — KITCHEN SET

Cabinet with sink and faucet (practical)	With catch basin under sink
Dish towel holder	On DS side
Glass door cupboard against US wall	Set at intermission
Kitchen breakfront	
4 shelves on top, 2 drawers and 2 lower cabinets	
Refrigerator with practical light	Set at intermission
Stove with practical (propane)	DSL burner
Small rectangular kitchen table	
2 kitchen chairs with tie-on cushions	
Red kitchen step stool	
Plastic bin for recycling against wall	

ACT TWO

On Dining Table:

lace table cloth	Accordion pleated on DS side table

On Kitchen Table:

2 flowers (carnations) in water
    pitcher
cutting board

Kitchen Stove:

ham (artificial) in roasting pan	Butt end facing DS
1 pot of hot water for macaroni	On DR practical burner on low
	(top of show — on burner offstage)
macaroni	Added at intermission

1 pot on UR burner—set dressing
    only
small brown crockery pot—dressing UC on stove
    only

In Fridge:
4 oranges (Act Three)
raw chicken wrapped in butcher paper
pre-mixed stuffing with glass bowl with spoon
cubed cheese (1/2 inch — approx. 36) in bowl
maraschino cherry jar — 2 used per performance
plastic bag with chopped parsley
1 glass pitcher with water
1 plate with 2 large pieces of coconut (Act Three)
misc. food stuffs as dressing

Upper Cabinet shelf Behind Glass Doors:
salt and pepper shakers
2 extract bottles (reset Act Three)
1 large box of salt with pour
    spout (reset Act Three)
baking powder (reset Act Three)
5 water glasses — actor 1 uses   On 2nd shelf SR
    for glass of water

Additional cabinet dressing includes:
3 assorted plastic bowls
box of matches
box of elbow macaroni 3/4 full
box of tissue
misc. canned goods

In Bottom Cabinet SL:
1 colander for macaroni   On top shelf
1 large glass casserole dish   On top shelf
    for chicken
plastic bag (for garbage)   Hung on interior of door

In Counter Drawer:
  2 wooden spoons
  1 rubber spatula
  1 large fork
  1 paring knife
  1 dish towel

On Counter Top:

Cutting board	DS of sink
4 turnips	On cutting board
1 cucumber with fork propped on it	US of sink
1 folded dish towel	On cutting board
2 chopping knives	On cutting board
1 vegetable peeler with black handle	In carrot bowl
1 brown bowl with four carrots	US of sink
1 cabbage (artificial) in bowl	US of sink
1 head cauliflower (artificial) in bowl	US of sink
1 bunch broccoli (2 if small)	US of sink
1 flour bin	Against back near stove
1 sugar bin	Against back/SL of flour
1 butter crock/bowl filled with butter	On top of celery container
1 plastic bowl with water	In sink
1 vegetable scrub brush	In bowl in sink
1 dish "Handi-wipe" towel on faucet	Back of sink
3 empty bowls	
yellow "sweet potato"	USL corner
white with blue rim "broccoli"	US of sink
1 light blue "turnip"	DS of sink
Sliced celery in covered container	US sink (under butter)

1 large can of condensed milk with 2 openings	SL of sugar bin
4 pot holders	Hanging from wall under cabinet
2 hot mitts	On top of flour and sugar bins
1 Pyrex measuring 2-cup with stock	DS of flour bin
1 wooden spoon	In stock cup
1 sauté pan — for gravy	Hanging SR of cabinet
1 sauté pan lid	Standing US behind pot holders
1 metal measuring cup with 1/3 cup flour	SL of flour/sugar bins
2 silver serving forks (for ham)	US of sink
1 rubber spatula	US of sink
1 wooden spoon	US of sink
1 large metal serving spoon	US of sink
*Red step stool with step out (with Sadie's apron)	SR of sink, facing DS
Bar of soap on sink	

KITCHEN BREAKFRONT SR:

Garbage can with foot opening lid with liner	SL of breakfront
Portable radio	SR lower shelf
Photo of Baby Hubie	CTR 2nd shelf
Photo of Hubert	CTR 2nd shelf
Corningware dish with cover–macaroni	SR 2nd shelf
Desert serving tray with 6 cups (Act Three)	CTR lower shelf
1 grater (Act Three) — coconut	In bottom cupboard SR
Bessie's apron with hankie	In SL drawer
Dish towels	

Additional breakfront dressing includes:
  misc. photos
  misc. letters and postcards
  mason jars (13)
  2 green glass vases
  large brown flowered platter
  spiral calendar propped up
  1 small rectangular metal tray
  blue and cream metal canister
  bear salt and pepper shakers
  corn salt and pepper shakers
  glass jar of cookies
  honey jar
  small floral vase
  glass sugar container
  floral metal canister
  painted green vase
  cream and green pie plate
  Twinings tea canister
  red and white square canister
  blue and white candlesticks
  brown and white floral canister
  old fan
  4 cookbooks
  needlework frame with holder
  Whitman's sampler candy box
  2 trivets

OFFSTAGE PRESETS — ACT TWO

Burlap bag of sweet potatoes (10, 6 taken out)	On near prop table SR
Unframed photo of Bessie "Brunswick"	In serving dish on prop table
Rectangular glass serving dish for cucumber	

Pineapple rings in covered plastic
    dish for ham
Toothpicks in shot glass to secure pineapple rings

ACT THREE — KITCHEN

On Table:

#2 cutting boards (from Act Two)	Larger board DSR
2 paring knives	
*4 naval oranges (from fridge Act Two)	2 on each board
1 glass bowl for peels	DC on table
1 red and white check towel	Actor pick up from SR prop table
1 terry cloth towel	SL on table

On Counter:

1 towel hanging from rack	
*1 white sugar bowl with spoon from Act Two	DS of sink
*2 bottles extract	DS of sink (from cabinet)
*1 large salt container	US sink (from cabinet)
*1 spice bottle of mace	US sink (from cabinet)
*1 can baking powder	US sink (from cabinet)
Flour mixing bowl	US Pyrex loaf pan
Large bowl with butter and wooden spoon	US sink
Mixing bowl with two eggs	US sink
*Butter crock (from Act Two)	US sink/SL baking disk
1 rectangular Pyrex baking loaf dish	US sink
1/2 folded paper towel in pan	To butter pan
*1 rubber spatula	DS of flour bin (from drawer)
*1 dinner fork	

*1 wooden spoon	DS of flour bin (from drawer)
*1 metal measuring cup (from Act Two, now empty)	SL of bins
*Plate of coconut (from earlier preset)	In fridge
*Desert tray (from earlier preset)	Moved to SL side of shelf

Living/Dining Room:

*Flower vase (from Act Two)	On dining table–USR of ham
*Dish of cucumber (from Act Two)	On dining table–DSR of ham
*Ham on platter (from Act Two)	On dining table–CTR
*3 photo albums (from before)	On bookshelf–SR
*Water tray and pitcher with 2 glasses	On bookshelf–CL
*Bible (from before)	On sitting table–DR

*Bessie's Jacket
Draped: onstage arm of Sadie's chair folded with shoulders together, open to DS and collar to SL

*Sadie's Shawl
Folded lengthwise, draped on Bessie's chair (check fold is down on seat for actor, laid over back of chair on diagonal)

ACT THREE OFFSTAGE

Cutglass bowl for ambrosia	On/near prop table

(*) denotes props listed in earlier preset.

Note: all food is real unless indicated as "artificial"

SCENE DESIGN
"HAVING OUR SAY"
LIVING ROOM
(DESIGNED BY THOMAS LYNCH FOR THE McCARTER THEATER)

SHOW PORTAL

SCRIM SHOW DROP

WINDOW

NO FRIDGE
ACT I

LOW BOOKCASES

TABLE

CHAIRS

TABLE
&
CHAIRS

SIDEBOARD

WINDOW

PRINTED
MASONITE

VELOUR
TO HERE

NOTES
(Use this space to make notes for your production)